OTHER BOOKS BY HELEN EXLEY

Be Brave!   Be Confident!   Be a Rebel!

Be You!   BELIEVE IN YOURSELF   Be Happy!

Friendship 365   HOPE! DREAM! LIVE! 365   Yes to life! 365

EDITED BY HELEN EXLEY
ILLUSTRATED BY JULIETTE CLARKE

Published in 2019 by Helen Exley®LONDON in Great Britain.
Illustrated by Juliette Clarke © Helen Exley Creative Ltd 2019.
Design and creation by Helen Exley © Helen Exley Creative Ltd 2019.
All the words by Odile Dormeuil, Pam Brown, Charlotte Gray, Maya V.
Patel, Hannah C. Klein, Pamela Dugdale, Linda Macfarlane, Stuart &
Linda Macfarlane copyright © Helen Exley Creative Ltd 2019.

12 11 10 9 8 7 6 5 4 3 2

ISBN : 978-1-78485-187-3

MIX
Paper from
responsible sources
FSC® C015559

Helen Exley®LONDON,
16 Chalk Hill, Watford, Herts WD19 4BG, UK
www.helenexley.com

Awesome
QUOTES
for
Strong
WOMEN

Helen Exley

W e should take pride in our femininity
and our feminine qualities –
warmth, nurturing, tenderness and caring.

JOAN COLLINS, B. 1933

Women are the rea

A ccept your womanhood,
and rejoice in it. It is your glory
that you are a woman.

PEARL S. BUCK 1892 – 1973

architects of society.

HARRIET BEECHER STOWE 1811 – 1896

Life is not easy for any of us.
But what of that?
We must have perseverance and
above all confidence in ourselves.
We must believe that we are gifted
for something,
and that this thing,
at whatever cost,
must be attained.

MARIE CURIE 1867 – 1934

A woman
is the full circle.
Within her
is the power
to create,
nurture,
and transform.

DIANE MARIECHILD

The most beautiful woman in the world is the one who protects and supports other women.

SANDRA BULLOCK, B. 1964

No woman is without sisters

however desperate,

however lacking in kin.

For all the women

of the world

are bound together

by common experience

and concern.

HANNAH C. KLEIN

Men went roaring round the world.
Waving their swords and shouting.
While women stayed home
and made a life
for them to come home to.
Very quietly
creating civilization.

PAM BROWN

Awoman kneads the bread
of the family, shaping it, warming it,
combining the ingredients
of different personalities.
From her doughy body,
she bears them;
with her stubborn hands
she forms them;
in the oven of her love,
she binds them together.
Her task is nothing less
than the creation of paradise.

DIANE ACKERMAN, B. 1948

Every woman
has a right
to be all
that she can be,
and to know all
she can know.

AUTHOR UNKNOWN

We have the opportunity to create
a new conversation with our ideas,
thoughts, passions, and skills –
one that is based not just
on the problems facing women
but on our joy,
confidence, and spirit as well.
Today we decide what we want,
and nothing is impossible.

PAULA GOLDMAN, B. 1975

Our home is the universe.
Our task is anything
we set our minds and hearts to.

MAYA V. PATEL 1943 – 2014

Women, I believe

can do anything.

NANCY KLINE, B. 1955

I wonder who made the first pot?

Sowed the first seed?

Sewed the first garment?

Made the cave comfortable?

Suggested things.

Healed wounds.

And raised the children?

PAM BROWN

Men,
their rights and nothing more;
Women,
their rights and nothing less.

SUSAN B. ANTHONY 1820 – 1906

Some women choose to follow men, and some women choose to follow their dreams. If you're wondering which way to go, remember that your career will never wake up and tell you that it doesn't love you anymore.

LADY GAGA, B. 1986

A man told me
that for a woman,
I was very
opinionated.
I said, "For a man,
you're kind of
ignorant."

ANNE HATHAWAY, B. 1982

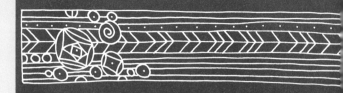

Just like diamonds grab the light
and refract it into the many colors
of the rainbow because of their facets,
we can capture the full potential
of our individual and collective power.
The facets reflect our truly phenomenal
nature as women.

HELEN LERNER-ROBBINS

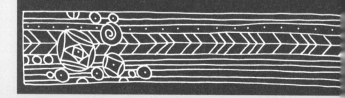

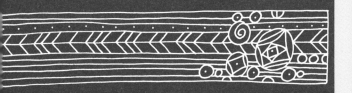

The success
of every woman
should be the inspiration
to another.
We should
raise each other up.

SERENA WILLIAMS, B. 1981

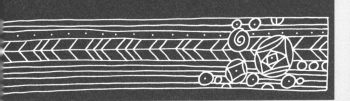

The female instinct in a strong,
true woman is imbued in all her brain
and body. Really feminine woman
cannot be and is not afraid to do
or be anything she likes.
She is woman.
Whatever she does is feminine and full
of woman, and she could not ape man
if she tried, for she is all woman

and all her thinking and breathing
and being are woman, and her femaleness
is herself and it cannot be taken
from her or be changed,
nor does she want to be changed.
She wants to be what she is,
a woman; and as a woman
she goes anywhere and does everything,
secure in her own content and being.

PEARL S. BUCK 1892 – 1973

WOMEN TOGETHER
FOR A NEW WORLD

You and I will fold the sheets
Advancing towards each other
From Burma, from Lapland,

From India where the sheets have been
washed in the river
And pounded upon stones:
Together we will match the corners.

From China where women on either side
of the river
Have washed their pale cloth in the White
Stone Shallows
"Under the shining moon".

We meet as though in the formal steps
of a dance
To fold the sheets together, put them to air
In wind, in sun over bushes, or by the fire.

We stretch and pull from one side and then
the other – Your turn. Now mine.
We fold them and put them away until they
are needed.

A wish for all people when they lie down
to sleep –
Smooth linen, cool cotton, the fragrance
and stir of herbs
And the faint but perceptible scent of sweet
clear water.

ROSEMARY DOBSON 1920 – 2012

This may look like a little girl,
but she's learning, she's preparing
to sprout the gifts that women-kind
have had since time began.
Watch out for signs.
The ability to be in two places at once.
Eyes in the back of her head.
A nose for danger.
The skill to kiss away a pain.
And make something out of nothing.
You have a Wonder Woman
on your hands.
Wait and watch and wonder.

PAM BROWN

When a woman rises up in glory, her energy is magnetic and her sense of possibility contagious.

MARIANNE WILLIAMSON, B. 1952

... dreams are important.
Without them, little girls
wouldn't grow up to be soccer stars,
chemical engineers, dog trainers,
actresses, even teachers.
They wouldn't travel in space,
defend our country in foreign lands
or represent us in government.

KRIS HAMM ROSS

What goes unsaid is that women
might be more ambitious and focused
because we've never had a choice.
We've had to fight to vote, to work outside
the home, to work in environments
free of sexual harassment, to attend
the universities of our choice, and we've
also had to prove ourselves over and over
to receive any modicum of consideration.

ROXANE GAY, B. 1974

Women are sowers
of the seeds
that will bring
peace and justice
into our world.

STUART & LINDA MACFARLANE

The word for "woman" is *soutoura*.
It refers to self-knowledge,
self-esteem,
and self-respect.
These are necessary
if one is to obtain the respect
of others,
something my mother regarded
as essential for a woman.

AMINATA TRAORÉ, B. 1942

We teach girls to shrink themselves,
to make themselves smaller.
We say to girls:
"You can have ambition, but not too much.
You should aim to be successful,
but not too successful.
Otherwise, you will threaten the man."
Because I am female, I am expected
to aspire to marriage.

I am expected to make my life choices,
always keeping in mind that marriage
is the most important.
Now, marriage can be a source of joy
and love and mutual support,
but why do we teach girls
to aspire to marriage
and we don't teach boys the same?

CHIMAMANDA NGOZI ADICHIE, B. 1977

To nourish children and raise them
against the odds is in any time,
any place, more valuable than to fix bolts
in cars or design nuclear weapons.

MARILYN FRENCH 1929 – 2009

Successful women...
take the initiative and assume extra
responsibilities. They have in common
the knack for turning sow's ears jobs
into silk-purse careers.

SUE HERERA

Women need to see ourselves
as individuals capable of creating change. That
is what political and economic power is about:
having a voice,
being able to shape the future.
Women's absence from decision making
positions has deprived us
of a necessary perspective.

MADELEINE KUNIN, B. 1933

It upsets me that women often gauge their self-worth on whether they are attractive to men. I think it's sad that women feel stronger and secure and worthy if they can attract men.

OK I admit that I do get a charge if I walk into a room and I notice that some heads turn. It's still a little bit of a boost

and you can't help that. But I would hate
the day that I thought that because men
were not looking at me anymore,
I had no worth or purpose.
I think that is the problem for women
and that is why they fear ageing –
because they gauge themselves
through the men they attract.

GOLDIE HAWN, B. 1945

*Educate a woman
and you educate
her family.
Educate a girl
and you change
the future.*

QUEEN RANIA AL-ABDULLAH
OF JORDAN, B. 1970

Dear Sirs, man to man, manpower, craftsman, working men, the thinking man, the man in the street, fellow countrymen, the history of mankind, one-man show, man in his wisdom, statesman, forefathers, masterful, masterpiece, old masters, the brotherhood of man, Liberty, Equality, Fraternity, sons of free men, faith of our fathers, god the father, god the son, yours fraternally, amen. Words fail me.

STEPHANIE DOWRICK

A strong woman artist
who is not afraid of herself,
her sexuality, passion, symbols,
language, who is fearless, willing
to take any and all risks,
often produces work that is
staggeringly beautiful
and at the same time frightening,
dangerous, something
to be reckoned with.

LAURA FARABOUGH

What is truly indispensable for the conduct
of life has been taught us by women —
the small rules of courtesy, the actions
that win us the warmth or deference of others;
the words that assure us a welcome;
the attitudes that must be varied to mesh
with character or situation;
all social strategy. It is listening to women
that teaches us to speak to men.

REMY DE GOURMONT 1858 – 1915

Give me
a place
to stand
and I can
move
the world.

ARIANNA HUFFINGTON, B. 1950

The great women of the past –
and there have been many –
had more to contend with than we do.
Yet many of us still feel that it is
too hard to accomplish our goals,
or hesitate to act because we fear
that we might fail.
We forget that everything
starts with a single, small step.

ZOE SALLIS

It has barely
begun,
the search
of women
for themselves.

BETTY FRIEDAN 1921 – 2006

For women there are, undoubtedly
great difficulties in the path,
but so much the more
to overcome.
First no woman should say,
"I am but a woman!"
But a woman!
What more can you ask to be?

MARIA MITCHELL 1818 – 1889

The two important things I did learn
were that you are as powerful
and strong as you allow yourself to be,
and that the most difficult part
of any endeavour
is taking the first step,
making the first decision.

ROBYN DAVIDSON

The great women
of the world started small.
They had a lifetime
and they filled it full.
Took what they had
and used it.
Left something good behind.

ODILE DORMEUIL

W omen will always fear war
more than men because
they are mothers. A woman
will always have a baby,
her own or her children's
in her arms. She will always
be tormented by fear for her
children, the fear that one day
she might be a witness
to their own deaths.

NATALAYA BARANSKAYA
1908 – 2004

Everything that gives birth
is female.
When men begin to understand
the relationships
of the universe that women
have always known,
the world will begin
to change for the better.

LORRAINE CANOE

Man may work from sun to sun, but women's work is never done.

In the book Soldiers on the Home Front, I was greatly struck by the fact that in childbirth alone, women commonly suffer more pain, illness and misery than any war hero ever does. And what's her reward for enduring all that pain? She gets pushed aside when she's disfigured by birth, her children soon leave, her beauty is gone. Women, who struggle and suffer pain to ensure the continuation of the human race, make much tougher and more courageous soldiers than all those big-mouthed freedom-fighting heroes put together.

ANNE FRANK 1929 – 1945

Sit down and ask yourself,
'What is the most important thing to me?'
What grosses me out the most?
What makes me the most upset —
is it healthcare? Is it so many people
being hungry in our culture?
Is it sexual abuse? Mix that with doing
something you love, something you
could keep doing forever and ever.

For me it was ending violence against
women, and I mixed it with music.
And I've had a twenty-five-year career.
So that's my advice:
Find something you really care about and mix
that with something you love doing.

KATHLEEN HANNA, B. 1968

Every time one of us achieves success, we all profit.

HELEN LERNER-ROBBINS

What makes a successful businesswoman?
Is it talent? What is the mystical ingredient?
It's persistence. It's that certain little spirit
that compels you to stick it out just when
you're at your most tired.
It's that quality that forces you to persevere,
find the route around the stone wall.
It's the immovable stubbornness
that will not allow you to cave in
when everyone says give up.

ESTÉE LAUDER 1908 – 2004

Women
pick up
the pieces
and repair
the world.

PAM BROWN

The bond between
women is a circle —
we are together within it.

JUDY GRAHN

...I think that women
would accomplish more if they would
worry less about what some men
or some commercials say...
and worry more about just being proud
to be a woman...

JENNIFER JOHNSON

When women stretch
to reach new levels of success
in both our personal
and professional lives,
we are able to achieve important
and wonderful things...
when we work together,
we can move the world.

NITA M. LOWEY

The thing women
have yet to learn is
nobody gives you power.
You just take it.

ROSEANNE BARR, B. 1952

Women can change the world.
We do not have to change men first.
We only have to lead them back
into our culture. Men will change
when they live inside women's culture
long enough to rediscover
the interactive selves they lost
as a result of male conditioning.

NANCY KLINE, B. 1955

At work, you think of
the children you have left at home.
At home, you think of the work
you've left unfinished.
Such a struggle is unleashed
within yourself.
Your heart is rent.

GOLDA MEIR 1898 – 1978

For women to put our hopes
and desires into words
is still a magical and rebellious
thing in spite of how common
it may seem to be. To have the freedom
to push our ideas and words further
than they have in the past is a gift
many women before
us have not been able to savor
(and many still cannot).

JEWELLE GOMEZ, B. 1948

Be wicked,
be brave,
be drunk,
be reckless,
be dissolute,
be despotic,
be an anarchist,
be a suffragette,
be anything you like —
but for pity's sake
be it to the top of your bent.

VIOLET TREFUSIS 1894 – 1972

Men resent women because women bear kids, and seem to have this magic link with immortality that men lack. But they should stay home for a day with a kid; they'd change their minds.

TUESDAY WELD, B. 1943

Unless a woman is very strong-minded or very rich, she has to fit her ambition around the housework.

HANNAH C. KLEIN

Humor is such a strong weapon, such a strong answer. Women have to make jokes about themselves, laugh about themselves, because they have nothing to lose.

AGNÈS VARDA 1928-2019

I think the best role models for women are people who are fruitfully and confidently themselves.

MERYL STREEP, B. 1949

Women are
the glue
that hold our
day-to-day
world together.

ANNA QUINDLEN, B. 1953

One of the wonderful things
about women,
which I don't think
social anthropologists have
fully understood,
is that we are bonded
by shared experiences.

ANITA RODDICK 1942 – 2007

I have yet to hear a man
ask for advice on how to combine
marriage and a career.

GLORIA STEINEM, B. 1934

I have chosen
to no longer
be apologetic
for my femaleness
and my
femininity.

CHIMAMANDA NGOZI ADICHIE, B. 1977

Women will talk to women anywhere,
anytime. Old Friends.
Slight acquaintances. Total strangers.
Bus queues. Underground trains.
Grocer shops. It's the mechanism
by which the world spins.

CHARLOTTE GRAY

The natural woman
loves and understands man
far too well...
She knows...
that without her
he is a poor, weak,
miserable,
buttonless creature.

MRS FANNY DOUGLAS

Women have a way
of treating people
more softly.
We treat souls
with kid gloves.

SHIRLEY CAESAR, B. 1938

The fundamental reason that women
do not achieve so greatly as men is that
women have no wives.

MARJORIE NICOLSON

Women never have a half-hour
in all their lives (excepting before or after
anybody is up in the house)
that they can call their own,
without fear of offending or of
hurting someone. Why do people sit up
so late, or, more rarely, get up so early?
Not because the day is not long enough
but because they have
"no time for themselves".

FLORENCE NIGHTINGALE 1820 – 1910

It is women enlisting,
educating and protecting women
who are bringing about the greatest
changes of this century.

NELLY MNISI

There was a time when war was
our survival. Now war is our demise.
Let it begin in the hearts of all women.
We hold the true power.

SCOUT CLOUD LEE, B. 1944

Think like a queen.
A queen is not afraid
to fail. Failure is
another stepping
stone to greatness.

OPRAH WINFREY, B. 1954

How brave men have been
in destruction. How brave women
have been in survival.

PAMELA DUGDALE

I'm furious about the Women's
Liberationists. They keep getting up on
soapboxes and proclaiming that women
are brighter than men.
That's true, but it should be kept quiet
or it ruins the whole racket.

ANITA LOOS 1893 – 1981

If you allow them,
women bring out their true self,
which is strong and talented
and powerful.
But the world didn't want to know
about that. The world wanted
to keep women down.

YOKO ONO, B. 1933

Yes, I am wise,
but it's wisdom full of pain.
Yes I've paid the price,
but look how much I've gained.
I am wise,
I am invincible,
I am Woman.

HELEN REDDY 1941 – 2020

The world has never yet seen
a truly great and virtuous nation,
because in the degradation
of women the very fountains of life
are poisoned at their source.

LUCRETIA MOTT 1793 – 1880

The spirit of womanhood –
a pure and beautiful thing and quite,
quite inviolate.

MONA BAUWENS & PETER THOMPSON

Whether eighteen or eighty –
whether single, mother or gran –
no matter race or creed –
a common bond unites all women.
They share the same hopes, fears,
joys and sorrows.
They understand each other's love,
peace and pain.
Their bond stretches around the globe
nurturing it by the power of their love.

LINDA MACFARLANE, B. 1953

You've got to rattle your cage door.
You've got to let them know
that you're in there,
and that you want out.
Make noise.
Cause trouble.
You may not win right away,
but you'll sure have a lot more fun.

FLORYNCE KENNEDY 1916 – 2000

All women hustle.
Women watch faces,
voices, gestures,
moods. She's
the person who
has to survive
through cunning.

MARGE PIERCY, B. 1936

The state of the world today demands that women become less modest and dream/plan/act/risk.

CHARLOTTE BUNCH, B. 1944

Women as a class have never subjugated another group; we have never marched off to wars of conquest in the name of the fatherland. We have never been involved in a decision to annex the territory of a neighboring country, or to fight for foreign markets on distant shores. These are the games men play, not us. We want to be neither oppressors nor oppressed. The women's revolution is the final revolution of them all.

SUSAN BROWNMILLER, B. 1935

You have been born into a world full
of dangers, but nevertheless a world
full of opportunities –
far greater than women
have ever known before.
You will need luck and determination
as well as intelligence and skills –
but there's at least a chance
for you now – a chance denied
your female ancestors.
For their sake, as well as for your own,
take the chances.
Follow your star.

PAM BROWN

Women are always being tested...
but ultimately, each of us
has to define
who we are individually
and then do the very best job
we can to grow into that.

HILLARY RODHAM CLINTON, B. 1947

We never really give ourselves credit.
We need to be able to say to ourselves,
"We can do it!"

PAT HARRISON

Look, I'm just trying to put something
good out into the world, it's not
going to solve patriarchy forever and ever.

TAVI GEVINSON, B. 1996

The worser effect on both man
and woman is found where woman's
acceptance of insult, having grown
mechanical, is eventually unconscious.

ELIZABETH ROBINS

Women understand the problems
of the nation better than men,
for women have solved the problems
of human life from embryo to birth
and from birth to maturity.
Women are the survival kit
of the human race.

COUNCILLOR MANDIZVIDZA

I'm a feminist.
I've been a female
for a long time now.
It'd be stupid
not to be
on my own side.

MAYA ANGELOU
1928 – 2014

Being nice should never be perceived
as being weak. It's not a sign of weakness,
it's a sign of courtesy, manners, grace,
a woman's ability to make everyone feel
at home, and it should never
be construed as weakness...

BENAZIR BHUTTO 1953 – 2007

...there is something about a gathering
of women around a kitchen table,
coffee cups in saucers, the windows open in
the breeze, the sound of quiet conversation,
and the mutuality of laughter.

MARGARET PERRON

The talent of women for communion, nurturing, and intuitive action has never been more needed than now, as we strive to meet the diverse cultural and environmental challenges of our times.

CAROL SPENARD LA RUSSO

We women have always been the ones to construct and piece together sanctuary and refuge for all our people – our neighbourhoods, our family.

JUNE JORDAN 1936 – 2002

The best
protection
any woman
can have is
courage.

ELIZABETH CADY STANTON

1815 – 1902

My advice to other women who have visions or passions and want to pursue them is: Pursue them, pursue them, pursue them, by all means, with eyes wide open as to the sacrifices necessary to live your vision and the incalculable rewards. We all have our particular gift to share with this world. If we ignore our gift, through insecurities, or fear, or even laziness, we cheat the world of hearing our voice and knowing our unique process.

MONICA PRABAR PILAR

If you retain nothing else,
always remember
the most important rule of beauty,
which is: Who cares?

TINA FEY, B. 1970

Don't forsake your own wisdom
because you fear you
will lose something.
What is more important?
Losing your face,
or losing your integrity?

GOLDIE HAWN, B. 1945

A liberated woman
is one who feels confident in herself,
and is happy in what she is doing.
She is a person who has a sense of self...
It all comes down to
freedom of choice.

BETTY FORD 1918 – 2011

I wish I could just go tell all the
young women I work with, all these fabulous
women, "Believe in yourself and negotiate
for yourself. Own your own success."

SHERYL SANDBERG, B. 1969

Who knows of the possibilities of love when men and women share not only children, home, and garden, not only the fulfilment of their biological roles, but the responsibilities and passions of the work that creates the human future.

It has barely begun, the search of women for themselves.

BETTY FRIEDAN 1921 – 2006

The real definition of girl power
is having the strength to be vulnerable
and trusting.

JILL CUNIFF

However idolized women have been –
in fact they have been required
to be as tough as old boots.

CHARLOTTE GRAY

How far do you go?
Go the distance! Within each person
is the potential to build the empire
of her wishes, and don't allow anyone
to say you can't have it all.
You can – you can have it all
if you're willing to work.

ESTÉE LAUDER 1908 – 2004

Women do have a lot to contribute
to business. They've got a lot of charm,
charisma and common sense.
They're not so worried
about their ego,
they're not afraid to say
"I'm not sure how to do this."

DEBBIE MOORE, B. 1946

To be gentle
should not imply
that you are
a doormat.
A gentle woman
has a backbone.

PAMELA DUGDALE

Starting out, several things
sustained me.
One was my burning desire to make art.
Another was when I realised
what women before me
had gone through in order for me
to have the opportunities that I had.

JUDY CHICAGO, B. 1939

Only you can know
how much you can give
to every aspect of your life.
Try to decide what is the most
important. And if you do,
then only occasionally
will you resent or regret
the demands of the marriage,
the career, or the child,
or the staying.

BARBARA WALTERS, B. 1929

It is a real fact that wherever
you want anything done,
teach a woman how to do it
and in a few days you will have
the same thing in various beautiful
uncountable numbers.

COUNCILLOR RUSHWAYA

Women speaking up for themselves and for those around them is the strongest force we have to change the world.

MELINDA GATES

My mother will take a deep breath
and straighten her shoulders,
"Daughter," she will say,
in a voice that is stern and admonishing,
"always a woman must be stronger
than the most terrible circumstance.
You know what my mother used to say?
Through us, the women of the world,
only through us
can everything survive."

KIM CHERNIN, B. 1940

When people say,
"Oh, you play strong women," I smile.
I know women are strong.
They're mothers,
they hold the family together,
they do 50 zillion things at once.
To be a single parent is much harder
than fighting an alien...
To me women are stronger than men.
But we keep it a big secret.

SIGOURNEY WEAVER, B. 1949

Most of us have trouble juggling. The woman who says she doesn't is someone whom I admire but have never met.

BARBARA WALTERS, B. 1929

My great hope is that at this marvellous
moment for women, they should remember
that one of the gifts they have is that they
remained so very close to the personal life,
and that the qualities that were discovered
in the personal life, the value of human life,
the value of tenderness, the attentiveness
to others' moods, the need for compassion
and pity and understanding, the things
that women practice every day
in their daily lives, in their small kingdoms,
are enormously important.

ANAÏS NIN 1903 – 1977

Women know that the best things in life are free. Caring, loving, understanding, supporting and comforting. All the things they give daily, continually, without asking for anything in return.

LINDA MACFARLANE, B. 1953

The men who espoused unpopular causes
may have been considered misguided,
but they were rarely attacked for their morals
or their masculinity. Women who did
the same thing were apt to be
denounced as harlots or condemned
for being unfeminine – an all-purpose
word that was used to describe
almost any category of female behavior
of which men disapproved.

MARGARET TRUMAN 1924 – 2008

Feminine power is having the confidence to be yourself. That is the most important thing for me. Confidence is power; it's huge power and if you're just calmly confident it's one of the most powerful things you can be.

AMANDA WAKELEY

The male is a biological accident:
the Y (male) gene is an
incomplete X (female) gene,
that is, has an incomplete set
of chromosomes.
In other words, the male is
an incomplete female...

VALERIE SOLANAS 1936 – 1988

Every woman should be the absolute mistress of her own body.

MARGARET SANGER 1879 – 1966

Women measure their achievements
not in the wealth they have gathered
but in the love
they have gathered around them.

LINDA MACFARLANE, B. 1953

Women have been abused,
misused and the appendages
of men for centuries,
and now we finally have an
opportunity to be ourselves.

JOAN COLLINS, B. 1933

No one sex can govern alone. I believe
that one of the reasons why civilization
has failed so lamentably is that it has had
one-sided government.

LADY NANCY ASTOR 1879 – 1964

I came very late to the women's mafia,
which is our answer to the old boys' network.
Theirs starts at school; we have to build
ours subsequently.

BARONESS JEAN DENTON 1935 – 2001

I think we need to stop giving men
cookies for doing what they should do.

CHIMAMANDA NGOZI ADICHIE, B. 1977

Once you live with the issue of women
and the landscape for a while, you find
that you cannot separate them from
the notions of peace, spirituality,
and community. As women we must learn
to become leaders in society, not just for
our own sake, but for the sake of all people.
We must support and protect our kinship
with the environment for the generations
to come.

CHINA GALLAND

Who knows
what women
can be when they
are finally
free to become
themselves.

BETTY FRIEDAN 1921 – 2006

If there is a great opportunity
within twenty feet, grab it and worry later
about whether you seemed pushy,
inappropriate, or overly eager.

KATE WHITE, B. 1951

If you want anything said, ask a man.
If you want anything done, ask a woman.

BARONESS MARGARET THATCHER
1925 – 2013

The fact is, I can have any experience of life I want. I don't have to choose any one thing or act in any one way to define myself as a woman now. I am one.

ALLY SHEEDY, B. 1962

Social science affirms that a woman's place in society marks the level of civilization.

ELIZABETH CADY STANTON
1815 – 1902

Women carry the puzzle of family life in their heads, they just automatically do: birthdays, presents, wrapping paper, holidays, medical appointments, name-tags, moving house, moving the sofa to a better spot, kitchen roll, nits, jabs, the need for new shoes, a bigger car-seat, a haircut.

ALLISON PEARSON, B. 1960

"If more women were in power,
they wouldn't let wars break out,"
she said. "Women can't be bothered
with all this fighting. We see war
for what it is – a matter of broken bodies
and crying mothers."

ALEXANDER MCCALL SMITH, B. 1948

I look at women as a metaphor
for what this world is going through.
We're the life givers, we're the birthers.
If we ignore that,
well, look at the state of the planet.

CARRÉ OTIS, B. 1968

Why, then, do women need power?
Because power is freedom.
Power allows us to accomplish
what is important to us, in the manner
that we best see fit. It separates
the doers from the dreamers.

PATTI F. MANCINI

Women, as the guardians of children,
possess great power. They are the moulders
of children's personalities
and the arbiters of their development.

ANN OAKLEY

I love being a woman. You can cry.
You get to wear pants now.
If you're on a boat
and it's going to sink,
you get to go
on the rescue boat first.
You get to wear cute clothes.

GILDA RADNER 1946 – 1989

Women are expected
to do twice as much
as men in half
the time and for
no credit.
Fortunately this
isn't difficult.

CHARLOTTE WHITTON

The woman is not needed to do man's work. She is not needed to think man's thoughts... Her mission is not to enhance the masculine spirit, but to express the feminine; hers is not to preserve a man-made world, but to create a human world by the infusion of the feminine element into all of its activities.

MARGARET SANGER 1879 – 1966

The struggle for equality
continues unabated,
and the woman warrior
who is armed with wit
and courage
will be among the first
to celebrate the victory.

MAYA ANGELOU 1928 – 2014

We rule the world – men just
haven't figured that out yet.

PAMELA ANDERSON, B. 1967

I think you can
be defiant and
rebellious and
still be strong
and positive.

MADONNA, B. 1958

I can tell you that whenever there
is a woman leader
at the helm of affairs, they face it
with courage and determination...

KHALEDA ZIA

We've always known – I guess
it's a secret among women – that we
have a lot of influence and that
we're pretty powerful.

LUCKY ROOSEVELT

There cannot be too many glorious women.
There cannot be too many queens.
There cannot be too much success.

MARIANNE WILLIAMSON, B. 1952

Men pay a heavy price for their
reluctance to encourage self-help and
independent resources in women.

GEORGE ELIOT (MARY ANN EVANS)
1819 – 1880

Women have always been allowed
to be clever and able – as long as they kept
very quiet about it.

ODILE DORMEUIL

I became a feminist because
I wanted to help my daughters,
other women and myself
aspire to something more
than a place behind a good man.

FAITH RINGGOLD, B. 1930

I myself have never been able to find out precisely what feminism is: I only know that people call me a feminist whenever I express sentiments that differentiate me from a doormat.

DAME REBECCA WEST 1892 – 1983

I just love bossy women…
To me, bossy… means somebody's passionate and engaged and ambitious and doesn't mind leading.

AMY POEHLER, B. 1971

...woman is the teacher
of man and children,
without her there is no one
to share the spirit of life.

BRID FITZPATRICK

The laughter of women together
is so revealing. It is the recognition of
freedom and friendship.

ANITA RODDICK 1942 – 2007

The practice of putting women on pedestals began to die out when it was discovered that they could give orders better from that position.

BETTY GRABLE 1915 – 1973

The first problem for all of us, men and women, is not to learn, but to unlearn.

GLORIA STEINEM, B. 1934

I think
the key is
for women
not to set
any limits.

MARTINA NAVRATILOVA, B. 1956

I'm thrilled that women are encouraged to follow their dreams and I am equally pleased that young men are getting a new view of women: an unapologetic woman.

LUCY LAWLESS

Because of their age-long training in human relations – for that is what feminine intuition really is – women have a special contribution to any group...

MARGARET MEAD 1901 – 1978

Ladies, unite. Let us cherish
our freaks and fanatics,
cultivate our obsessions,
hone our anger to a fine point
and never, never, listen to anyone
who says "be reasonable".

JILL TWEEDIE 1936 – 1993

Women are all

one nation.

TURKISH PROVERB

I've always believed that one woman's success
can only help another woman's success.

GLORIA VANDERBILT 1924 – 2019

The especial genius of women
I believe to be electrical in movement,
intuitive in function...

MARGARET FULLER 1810 – 1850

Women have served all these centuries as
looking-glasses possessing the magic
and delicious power of reflecting the figure
of man at twice its natural size.

VIRGINIA WOOLF 1882 – 1941

Men are not the enemy,
but the fellow victims.
The real enemy is
women's denigration
of themselves.

BETTY FRIEDAN 1921 – 2006

The women
hold the world
together.
And always
have.
And always
will.

ODILE DORMEUIL